Published by Creative Paperbacks
123 South Broad Street, Mankato, Minnesota 56001
Creative Paperbacks is an imprint of The Creative Company

Designed by Stephanie Blumenthal
Production Design by Melinda Belter

Photographs by Jay Ireland & Georgienne Bradley, Larry Merz,
A. B. Sheldon, Michael Turco, Doris VanBuskirk, and KAC Productions

Library of Congress Cataloging-in-Publication Data

Weir, Diana Loiewski.
Tree frogs / by Diana Loiewski Weir.
p. cm.
ISBN 0-89812-325-9

1. Hylidae—Juvenile literature. [1. Tree frogs. 2. Frogs.] I. Title.
QL668.E24 W45   2001
597.8'78—dc21   00-064335

First Paperback Edition

2 4 6 8 9 7 5 3 1

TREE FROGS

DIANA LOIEWSKI WEIR

CREA TIVE
PAPER BACKS

FROG

Frogs and toads may have been the first backboned land animals with a voice.

4

rogs are some of nature's most fascinating creatures. Of the 4,000 species of frogs, about 450 belong to a group called *hylidae*—skilled climbers that spend most of their lives off the ground high in trees.

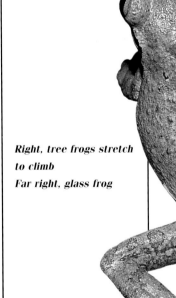

Right, tree frogs stretch to climb
Far right, glass frog

FROG
COUPLE

The female tree frog is more than twice the size of the male.

Above, vernal pool
Right, White's tree frog

FROGS AS AMPHIBIANS

Like all **amphibians**, tree frogs have two distinct life stages: they are born in the water, then grow to become land-dwelling adults. The first stage of life for a tree frog is the tadpole stage. A tadpole lives in ponds and pools of water, eating plants and algae. It has a long tail and no limbs. The tadpole experiences the process of **metamorphosis**, or change, at around four weeks of age, when the tail begins to shrink up into the body and front and back limbs begin to emerge. Lungs gradually develop to replace the gills. Once the limbs and lungs are fully formed, the tree frog is considered an adult and leaves the water to find a home in a forest or jungle **habitat**.

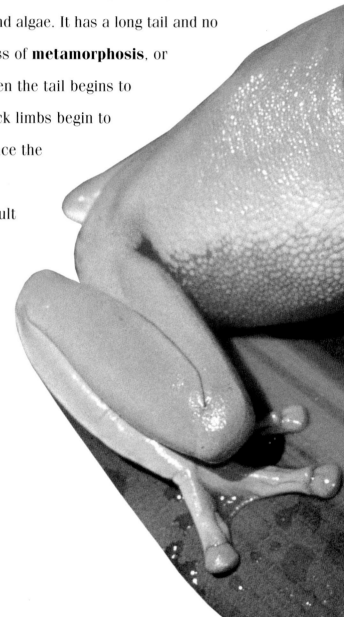

BELIEVE IT

Some tree frogs can fly from tree to tree in the rain forests.

OR NOT

Flying frogs don't actually fly; they merely glide— some up to 50 feet (15.2 m)!

Large orange tree frog

FROG
F A C T

Tree frogs can breathe in three different ways: through their mouths, their noses, and their skin.

Red-backed poison frog

L ike all amphibians, the tree frog is ektothermic. This means it must rely on the temperature of the surrounding environment to warm up or cool down. An amphibian must sit in the sun to make itself warm, and then withdraw into a shady area to cool its body down. Too much sun will dehydrate and literally bake an amphibian to death, so shade is vital to its survival.

FROG
F A C T

A frog's tongue is about as long as its head. If straightened, a tree frog's back legs would be longer than its body.

FROG
S M E L L

A tree frog's nose is near the tip of its face. Scientists believe that tree frogs can smell their prey.

Green and black poison frog

Because a tree frog is ektothermic, its body temperature slowly lowers as the environment becomes colder. As the seasons change, the frog will gradually adjust to the cooler temperature and take refuge underground, in decayed parts of trees, or under **leaf litter** in order to conserve energy.

Amazingly, some species of tree frogs have been known to freeze solid in cold winter months—their bodies hard as rocks—and then revive in the warmth of spring to live as though nothing had happened to their bodies during the winter.

FROG
THIRST

Red-eyed tree frogs

TREE FROG FEET

The tree frog has other fascinating characteristics, including the kind of toes that make life high above the ground possible for these small animals. Though each species varies in size from three-quarters of an inch up to four inches (1.9–10.2 cm) in body length, all tree frogs have one thing in common: strong gripping toes capable of supporting the body vertically on a climbing surface.

The secret to the tree frog's amazing toes are the suction cup-shaped discs located at the ends. Secreting from the skin a wet, sticky film called **mucous**, tree frogs can scale the smoothest of surfaces—even glass—with the greatest of ease.

Because the tree frog's skin is highly sensitive, it can feel with its toes exactly where to step and on what spot to grip. This also comes in handy when hunting for food. Even the lightest touch alerts a tree frog to nearby prey.

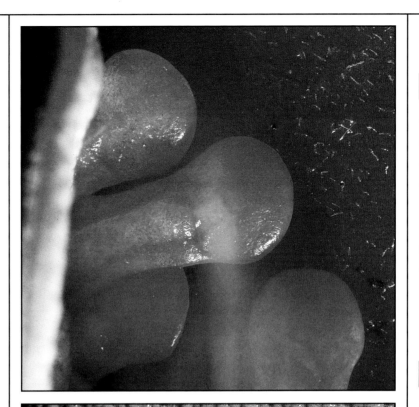

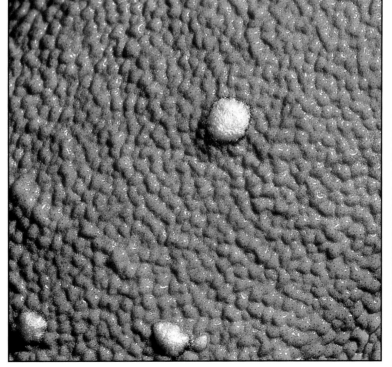

FROG
HISTORY

About 350 million years ago, amphibians evolved from lobe-finned fish. The tadpole, which breathes through gills and has no legs, resembles these fish.

FROG
FREEZE

Gray's tree frogs, wood frogs, and spring peepers have survived weeks of freezing with as much as 65 percent of their total body water as ice.

Top, toes of a red-eyed tree frog
Bottom, skin of a red-eyed tree frog

FROG
SIZE

The largest frog in the world is the Giganturana goliath of Africa, which can measure up to 39 inches (1 m) in body length; the smallest is the Sminthillus *at one-half inch (1.3 cm).*

Red-eyed tree frog

THE HUNTER AND THE HUNTED

Keen hearing and excellent distance vision also help the tree frog hunt. Frog eyes are located on the top and at the opposite sides of the head. This means that each eye has its own field of vision, allowing a tree frog to see in almost a complete circle. Any bug within tongue's length in any direction is a potential meal.

Unlike animals that chase food, frogs are patient and often wait for prey to come near them.

When hunting for prey, however, the frog will stalk silently and then make a surprise attack. Most kinds of tree frogs are graceful walkers and runners. Likewise, while stalking insects, a frog will fully extend its body as it steps carefully across leaves or stems. It will then stiffen and remain motionless for a time before continuing to patiently approach its intended meal.

FROG
HEARING

A tree frog's ears, which look like round discs, are behind its eyes. A tree frog can hear both on land and in the water.

Frog ears are shiny grayish discs

13

FROG

Most tree frogs can produce three calls: one that announces the frog's presence, an aggressive call, and a mating call.

FROG

JUMPS

The tree frog is an expert jumper; however, it's not so good at landing. To protect its eyes, it retracts them into its skull when jumping.

Right, frogs retract their eyes to swallow Opposite, giant monkey frog

Tree frogs don't have teeth—they don't need them. Rather, ridges in the upper and lower parts of the mouth hold the meal while it is swallowed whole. To swallow, the tree frog retracts, or pulls back, its eyes into its skull and uses them to push the prey down the throat.

The frog's tongue, attached at the front of the mouth and facing backward, also helps to push food down the throat. A hungry tree frog will attack anything small, from worms and beetles to butterflies and even hornets.

FROG
TRAVELER

The marine toad was moved from Mexico to the sugar cane fields of Australia to help control insects.

*Above, white tree frog
Right, a perfect frog breeding area*

REPRODUCTION AND GROWTH

While frogs spend a lot of time eating, they don't even think about food during mating season. In the spring, male tree frogs return to water for breeding. To attract females, the males make loud calls. Each species has its own unique call. For example, Gray's tree frog makes a repeating trill sound, the barking tree frog makes an *ark-ark* sound, and the spring peeper is named after its call, a high *peep*.

FROG
SQUISHY

Tree frogs do not have ribs, which explains why their bodies are so soft.

FROG
F A C T

Chorus frogs are tree frogs, but unlike their relatives they have short toe webs and small discs; they climb only on low shrubbery.

Left, expanding the throat to croak

Attracted by the male's call, a female tree frog will follow the sound to the body of water where mating will take place. By this time of the year, the female's body is already filled with eggs. She enters the water and selects a male of her species with which to mate. He climbs onto her back, and as the female releases her eggs into the water, the male **fertilizes** them so they will develop. The female lays hundreds of eggs in jelly-like clumps, often on a twig or grassy area in the water to protect them from hungry fish.

FROG

A few tree frog species don't return to water to breed. The male of these species summons a female to a tree with his call. Once there, the female finds a branch overhanging a pond or swamp and spreads a body fluid onto it. She kicks this fluid, literally whipping up a foam nest. She then lays her eggs into the nest, and the male fertilizes them as they are released. The placement of the nest is extremely important because as the eggs hatch, the fragile tadpoles need to drop into the water below.

Each egg contains a tiny tadpole

D
epending upon the species, frog eggs hatch in six to eight days. A tadpole looks and acts more like a fish than a frog, which is why during this stage of life, the tadpole must live in a pool of water to survive. Its diet consists of plants and algae, though sometimes a tadpole will help keep a pond clean by eating pieces of dead animals decaying on the pond floor. As the tadpole grows, its tail is absorbed into its body, providing nourishment as well.

FROG
SNACK

Unlike snakes, which leave their shedded skin behind, frogs eat the skin they shed.

Left, nest of a glass tree frog
Above, golden poison frog

FROG

NAME

Polliwog is another name for tadpole; poll means "head" and wog means "to wiggle."

FROG

DANGER

Scientists have found that frog eggs exposed to high amounts of ultraviolet (UV) radiation, as from too much direct sunlight, are weakened and do not develop properly.

Right, tadpoles need water to survive Opposite, common gray tree frog

Just as tadpoles rely on plants and algae for food, other animals rely on tadpoles to eat. Pond fish, such as trout, often prey on tadpoles, as do many species of aquatic birds and snakes.

Perhaps one of the tadpole's most fearsome predators is the dragonfly nymph. Before they develop wings, young dragonflies live in the same pools of water as tadpoles. They have voracious appetites, and the soft bodies of little tadpoles make hearty meals for these insects.

FROG
STICKY

*Mucous is also produced on the tree frog's belly, which helps the tree frog **adhere** to surfaces.*

FROG
NURSERY

The young of a tree frog relative, the marsupial frog, develop in a pouch in the skin of the mother's back.

Tadpoles on parent

Surviving tadpoles may grow to leave the water, but natural dangers aren't any less severe for adult frogs. In captivity, tree frogs can live 20 to 25 years. In the wild, however, tree frogs seldom survive half this long. Tree frogs are at the bottom of the **food chain**. This means that while they prey on only a few things, specifically insects, they can be eaten by many other animals. To protect themselves from predators, most tree frogs rely on **camouflage** to hide in their surroundings.

The adult tree frog is counter-shaded, which means that the color of its top side and bottom side are different. A snake climbing up a tree to look for a meal might miss a frog whose white belly would blend in with the sky. Coming down from the top of the tree, the snake might not notice the frog's dark back blended in with the tree bark.

Some species of frogs living among beautiful plants and flowers are also protected by camouflage, as their red, orange, or yellow bodies resemble flowers.

FROG
GROWTH

After some species of tree frog eggs hatch in the foam nest, the tadpoles develop into frogs without ever dropping into the water below.

23

Left, glass frog
Above, Cuban tree frog

FROG

The Australian Rheobatrachus silus, a tree frog relative, swallows its eggs, letting them mature in its stomach, and then coughs up completely developed baby frogs.

24

FROG

CRICKET

The cricket tree frog got its name from the fact that it doesn't climb well, but, just like a cricket, it can jump very far.

Yellow dart frog

Another way that frogs naturally protect themselves is the opposite of camouflage. Brilliant red and blue colorings may catch the eye of a predator, but the frogs will usually not be eaten. That's because the bright colors are actually a warning to predators to stay away from the frogs—they are **poisonous**.

Secreted from the frog's skin and covering its entire body, the poison leaves a terrible taste in the mouth of any animal trying to eat a poison frog. Predators quickly learn to avoid such meals in the future.

The most poisonous type of tree frog known to humans lives in the rain forests of South America. These frogs are in the family of *Dendrobatidae* and are often no longer than two inches (5 cm). Their bodies are incredibly colorful in patterns of blues, reds, yellows, oranges, and even black.

Frogs without poison or camouflage ability may simply flee a predator. Some tree frogs can spread out their front and back toes to reveal a webbing between them. Catching the air much like a parachutist, the frogs float safely to the ground.

25

*Left, azure poison frog
Above, Chinese "glyding" frog*

FROG
F U N

The red-eyed tree frog lays its eggs on leaves that hang over a pond. As the eggs hatch, the tadpoles slide down the leaves right into the water.

FROG
C R I S I S

Spring peepers are among the frogs that have been found deformed, having extra legs or no eyes.

Black and green poison arrow frog

FROGS ARE VALUABLE

Protecting tree frogs is vital because they are important to the balance of nature and they benefit humans. Tree frogs help people by eating insects, especially mosquitoes, which can carry dangerous diseases. Studies have shown that on an average evening a tree frog will eat more than 100 insects! Many species of frogs have even been brought to other countries to control damaging insect populations.

For hundreds of years, many South American native peoples have used dendrobites as a tool for hunting. The tree frogs' poison is placed on the tip of a bamboo splinter, which is then shot from a blowgun. The target of the hunt might be a monkey, sloth, bird, or some other tree-dwelling animal that is commonly eaten by the natives.

FROG
MEDICINE

Scientists have discovered that White's tree frog has natural medicines in its skin that can heal human cold sores.

Yellow frog

FROG

Cuban tree frogs are such aggressive eaters that food dropped into a captive frog's cage will be immediately snatched up in mid-air.

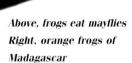

Today, the same poisons that were once used to kill are being used to heal. Studies of tree frog poisons are being conducted to find new kinds of medicines.

Unfortunately, while tree frogs could be used to save people, it may soon be too late to save tree frogs.

**Above, frogs eat mayflies
Right, orange frogs of
Madagascar**

FROG

Spring peepers are often less than one inch (2.5 cm) long, yet their high-pitched peep can be heard for great distances and is often mistaken for a cricket chirp.

Many frog populations are slowly declining. Some species are plagued with **deformities**, developing bodies with extra limbs or even with no eyes. Scientists believe that ecological catastrophes are to blame for these occurrences, which could be early signs of serious problems in the environment—problems that could eventually affect human lives.

Top, brown tree frog
Bottom, Madagascar tree frog
Opposite, "dyeing" poison arrow frog

More needs to be learned about frogs and the conditions of their habitats in order to ensure their survival. Everyday efforts to conserve and recycle materials can help preserve natural **vernal pools**. In addition, **deforestation**, the destruction of healthy wetlands and forests, must stop if we are to save frogs from **extinction**.

Only with healthy habitats in which to live can these amazing creatures continue to climb, leap, and glide through trees around the world.

Glossary

Animals with the ability to **adhere** to a surface can stick to the surface without falling off.

Amphibians are animals that usually breathe underwater as young but breathe air and live in or near water as adults.

Camouflage is a way of hiding from danger by appearing to be part of the environment.

The permanent removal or clearing away of wetlands, forests, or jungles is called **deforestation**.

Deformities are physical problems in the way that something grows.

Plants or animals suffer **extinction** when their species has died out completely and disappeared from the earth.

A male **fertilizes** a female's eggs with sperm during mating so that the eggs can develop into young.

The **food chain** is an order in nature in which plants are eaten by some animals and those animals are in turn eaten by species of other, often larger, animals.

A **habitat** is an environment where plants and animals naturally live and grow.

Leaves that have fallen from trees and covered the ground in layer upon layer over the seasons is called **leaf litter**.

When animals change, as tadpoles change into frogs, they go through a **metamorphosis**.

Mucous is a slimy or wet liquid formed in the body; a gland secretes, or produces, mucous.

Something that is **poisonous** contains deadly substances called **toxins** that can injure or even kill a person or animal when absorbed or eaten.

Vernal pools are natural depressions in the earth that hold water from March through May. Amphibians often lay eggs in these pools.

Index